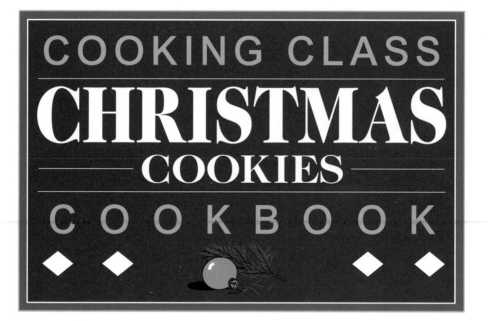

COOKING CLASS
CHRISTMAS
COOKIES
COOKBOOK

PUBLICATIONS INTERNATIONAL, LTD.

Recipe Development: Karen A. Levin, Lucy Wing

Photography: Sacco Productions Limited, Chicago

Pictured on the front cover: *(clockwise from top):* Polish Honey Bars *(page 60)*, Linzer Sandwich Cookies *(page 12)*, Christmas Ornament Cookies *(page 88)*, Argentinean Caramel-Filled Crescents *(page 10)* and Chocolate Madeleines *(page 38)*.
Pictured on the inside front cover: Moravian Spice Crisps *(page 22)*.
Pictured on the back cover: Danish Raspberry Ribbons *(page 28)*.

ISBN: 0-7853-1312-5

Manufactured in U.S.A.

8 7 6 5 4 3 2 1

CONTENTS

Christmas Spritz Cookies (page 72)

CLASS NOTES

Throughout the world, wherever Christmas is celebrated, getting together with family and friends and making cookies is a time-honored tradition. After all, cookie baking is the perfect holiday activity. People of all generations come together to make cookies, exchange recipes and share memories—and what gift is more heartfelt than a tin of homemade cookies?

While the word *cookie* comes to us from *koekje,* the Dutch word for little cakes, many believe the earliest cookies date back to 7th-century Persia. The Persians, one of the first groups to cultivate sugar, may have stumbled across these sweet treats while experimenting with their newly cultivated crops.

The cookie has evolved since the 7th century—an evolution due in part to its ability to adapt to its surroundings, making it easy for people of different countries to create traditional Christmas cookies from the spices, nuts, fruits and berries grown and harvested in their regions.

Not only are cookies created from the bounty of their native lands, but many have historical significance as well. One of Great Britain's most popular Christmas "biscuits," or cookies, is Shortbread (page 66). Shortbread, a rich, sand-textured, crisp cookie made with lots of butter, is baked in a round mold that dates back to the time of the ancient Druids. After baking, the mold (which is patterned to represent the sun's rays) turns out a single cookie that is cut into wedges prior to serving. Today, many types of shortbread molds are sold in cookware stores, including molds for individual cookies.

Germany is also famous for its *keks,* or cookies. Lebkuchen (page 44), the sacred cake, is one of the country's most popular. Bakers throughout Germany prepare the dough several weeks before Christmas to allow time for the dough to rest and the spices to blend. Once baked, the cookies are left to age, and the end result of the extended baking process is a soft cookie with a pleasantly mellow flavor.

The Germans were also the first group to produce Gingerbread Houses (page 85) and Gingerbread People (page 82). Although the tradition took more than 8,000 years to develop and many countries actively participated in the evolution of these decorative treats, they have since become a much-loved tradition in homes throughout the United States at Christmastime.

In Scandinavian countries, baking added a bit of sunshine and warmth to the dark and dreary days of winter. With such a lack of sunshine, it's no wonder Scandinavian bakers are world-famous for their cookie-baking skills. One of their most famous creations is the Christmas Spritz Cookie (page 72). These rich and buttery cookies, which are formed into a variety of fanciful shapes when the dough is "squirted" from a cookie press, get their name from the German word *spritzen,* which means to squirt.

Prior to the 1600s, honey was the only sweetener available in Europe—one reason why so many old world recipes call for honey instead of sugar. As the availability of sugar increased, it replaced honey in many recipes. However, because of Eastern Europe's ever-growing and influential honey industry, many cookies from the area, including Polish Honey Bars (page 60), are still made with honey today.

When the Spaniards arrived in the New World, they brought with them sugar cane and the technology to extract its juice. Soon, sugar was readily available. This made the production of Churros (page 68), an old Spanish favorite, and other cookies inevitable.

Another Spanish-speaking country famous for its cookies is Mexico. Its favorites include *pastelitos de boda,* better known as Mexican Wedding Cookies (page 50), and Mexican Sugar Cookies (page 52). They both fall into the category of *polvorones,* which means "sprinkled with powder," because they are coated with powdered sugar.

As you can see from our travel down the cookie time line, cookies have come a long way since their Persian ancestors. Despite their different names, these "little cakes," popular throughout the world, are treasured for their varied flavors and forms and are enjoyed by all as a tasty Christmas tradition.

GENERAL GUIDELINES

Ensure successful cookie baking by practicing these techniques:

• Read the entire recipe before you begin.

• Remove butter or margarine from the refrigerator to soften and eggs from the refrigerator to warm to room temperature, if necessary.

• Toast and chop nuts, peel and slice fruit and melt chocolate before preparing the dough.

• Measure all the ingredients accurately. Assemble them as directed in the recipe.

• When making bar cookies, use the pan size specified in the recipe and prepare the pan according to the recipe directions.

• Adjust oven racks if necessary and preheat the oven. Check the oven temperature for accuracy with an oven thermometer.

• Follow recipe directions and baking times. Check doneness with the test given in the recipe.

TYPES OF COOKIES

The seemingly endless variety of cookies can actually be divided into five basic types: bar, drop, refrigerator, rolled and shaped. These types are determined by the consistency of the dough and how it is formed into cookies.

Bar Cookies: Always use the pan size called for in the recipe. Using a different size will affect the cookies' texture; a smaller pan will give a more cakelike texture, while a larger pan will give a drier texture.

Before cutting, most bar cookies should cool in the pan on a wire rack until just warm. To make serving easier, remove a corner piece first, then remove the rest.

Drop Cookies: Cookies that are uniform in size and shape will finish baking at the same time.

Drop the dough from a measuring spoon about 2 inches apart onto cookie sheets to allow for spreading, unless the recipe directs otherwise.

Refrigerator Cookies: Always shape the dough into rolls before chilling. Shaping is easier if you first place the dough on a piece of waxed paper or plastic wrap. Before chilling, wrap the rolls securely in plastic wrap, or air may penetrate the dough and cause it to dry out.

Use gentle pressure and a back-and-forth sawing motion with a sharp knife when slicing the rolls. Rotating the roll while slicing also keeps one side from flattening.

Rolled Cookies: Chill the dough before rolling for easier handling. Remove only enough dough to work with at one time. Save any trimmings and reroll them all at once to prevent the dough from becoming tough.

Shaped Cookies: These cookies can be hand-shaped into balls or crescents or forced through a cookie press into more complex shapes.

If the recipe calls for a cookie press, do not try shaping the dough by hand unless the recipe states that you may do so. The consistency of the dough was formulated to work with a cookie press.

When using a cookie press, if your first efforts are not successful, just transfer the dough back to the cookie press and try again.

MEASURING INGREDIENTS

Dry Ingredients: Always use standardized "dry" measuring spoons and "dry" measuring cups. Fill the correct measuring spoon or cup to overflowing and level it off with a metal spatula.

Use dry measures to measure flour, brown sugar, granulated sugar, powdered sugar, peanut butter, chocolate chips, sour cream, yogurt, nuts, dried fruit, coconut, chopped fresh fruit, preserves and jams.

When measuring flour, lightly spoon it into a measuring cup, then level it off. Do not tap the measuring cup, as this will pack the flour.

When measuring brown sugar, pack the sugar by pressing it in the cup with the back of a spoon and level it off with a spatula. It should

be the shape of the cup when turned out.

Liquid Ingredients: Use a standardized "liquid" glass or plastic measuring cup with a pouring spout. Place the cup on a flat surface; fill to the desired mark, checking the measurement at eye level.

When measuring sticky liquids such as honey and molasses, grease the measuring cup or spray it with nonstick cooking spray before adding the liquid to make removal easier.

BAKING

The best cookie sheets to use are those with no sides or one or two short sides. These sheets allow the heat to circulate easily during baking and promote even browning.

For more even baking and browning, place only one cookie sheet at a time in the center of the oven. If the cookies begin to brown unevenly, rotate the cookie sheet from front to back halfway through the baking time.

When baking more than one sheet of cookies at a time, rotate the two sheets from top to bottom halfway through the baking time.

For best results, use shortening or nonstick cooking spray to grease cookie sheets. Or, line the cookie sheets with parchment paper; this will eliminate cleanup, bake the cookies more evenly and allow the cookies to cool right on the paper instead of using wire racks.

Allow cookie sheets to cool between batches, as the dough will spread too quickly if it is placed on a cookie sheet that is still hot.

To avoid overbaking the cookies, check them at the minimum baking time. If more time is needed, watch carefully to make sure that the cookies don't burn. It is usually better to slightly underbake cookies than to overbake them.

The following are some general guidelines that can be used to determine doneness for many types of cookies.

Bar Cookies: In fudgelike bar cookies, the surface appears dull and a slight imprint remains after gently touching the surface with your fingertip.

In cakelike bar cookies, a wooden toothpick inserted in the center comes out clean and dry.

Drop Cookies: The surface is lightly browned, and a slight imprint remains after gently touching the surface with your fingertip.

Refrigerator Cookies: The edges are firm, and the bottoms are lightly browned.

Rolled Cookies: The edges are firm, and the bottoms are lightly browned.

Shaped Cookies: The edges are lightly browned.

Many cookies should be removed from cookie sheets immediately after baking and placed in a single layer on wire racks to cool. Fragile cookies may need to cool slightly on the cookie sheets before being removed to wire racks to cool completely. Bar cookies may be cooled and stored in the baking pan. Refer to the directions in each recipe for specific removal guidelines.

STORAGE

Unbaked cookie dough can usually be refrigerated up to one week or frozen up to six weeks before using. Rolls of dough should be sealed tightly in plastic wrap; other doughs should be stored in airtight containers. Label

dough with baking information for convenience.

Store soft and crisp cookies separately at room temperature to prevent changes in texture and flavor. Keep soft cookies in airtight containers. If they begin to dry out, add a piece of apple or bread to the container to help them retain their moisture. If crisp cookies become soggy, heat undecorated cookies in a 300°F oven for 3 to 5 minutes or until crisp.

Store cookies with sticky glazes, icings and fragile decorations in single layers between sheets of waxed paper. Bar cookies may be stored in their own baking pan by simply covering the pan with foil or plastic wrap after the cookies have cooled.

As a rule, crisp cookies freeze better than soft, moist cookies. Rich, buttery bar cookies are an exception to this rule, since they freeze extremely well. Baked cookies can be frozen in airtight containers or plastic food storage bags up to three months. Meringue-based cookies do not freeze well, and chocolate-dipped cookies may discolor if frozen. Thaw frozen cookies, unwrapped, at room temperature.

Argentinean Caramel-Filled Crescents (Pasteles)

3 cups all-purpose flour
½ cup powdered sugar
1 teaspoon baking powder
¼ teaspoon salt
1 cup butter, cut into pieces
6 to 7 tablespoons ice water
½ package (14 ounces) caramel candies, unwrapped
2 tablespoons milk
½ cup flaked coconut
1 large egg
1 tablespoon water

1. Place flour, powdered sugar, baking powder and salt in large bowl; stir to combine. Cut butter into flour mixture with pastry blender or 2 knives until mixture forms pea-sized pieces. Add ice water, 1 tablespoon at a time; toss with fork until mixture holds together. Form dough into 2 discs; wrap in plastic wrap and refrigerate 30 minutes or until firm.

2. Meanwhile, melt caramels and milk in medium saucepan over low heat, stirring constantly; stir in coconut with spoon. Remove from heat; cool.

3. Working with 1 disc at a time, unwrap dough and place on lightly floured surface. Roll out dough with lightly floured rolling pin to ⅛-inch thickness.

4. Cut dough with floured 3-inch round cookie cutter. Gently press dough trimmings together; reroll and cut out more cookies.

5. Preheat oven to 400°F. Grease cookie sheets; set aside. Beat egg and 1 tablespoon water in cup.

6. Place ½ teaspoon caramel mixture in center of each dough round. Moisten edge of dough round with egg mixture. Fold dough in half; press edge to seal. Press edge with fork.

7. Place cookies on prepared cookie sheets; brush with egg mixture. Cut 3 slashes across top of each cookie with tip of utility knife.

8. Bake 15 to 20 minutes or until golden brown. Remove cookies with spatula to wire racks; cool completely. Store tightly covered at room temperature. These cookies do not freeze well. *Makes about 4 dozen cookies*

Step 3. Rolling out dough to ⅛-inch thickness.

Step 6. Placing caramel mixture in center of dough round.

Linzer Sandwich Cookies

1⅓ cups all-purpose flour
¼ teaspoon baking powder
¼ teaspoon salt
¾ cup sugar
½ cup butter, softened
1 large egg
1 teaspoon vanilla
Seedless raspberry jam

1. Place flour, baking powder and salt in small bowl; stir to combine.

2. Beat sugar and butter in medium bowl with electric mixer at medium speed until light and fluffy, scraping down side of bowl once. Beat in egg and vanilla. Gradually add flour mixture. Beat at low speed until dough forms, scraping down side of bowl once.

3. Form dough into 2 discs; wrap in plastic wrap and refrigerate 2 hours or until firm.

4. Preheat oven to 375°F. Working with 1 disc at a time, unwrap dough and place on lightly floured surface. Roll out dough with lightly floured rolling pin.

5. Cut dough into desired shapes with floured cookie cutters. Cut out equal numbers of each shape. (If dough becomes soft, cover and refrigerate several minutes before continuing.)

6. Cut 1-inch centers out of half the cookies of each shape. Gently press dough trimmings together; reroll and cut out more cookies. Place cookies 1½ to 2 inches apart on *ungreased* cookie sheets.

7. Bake 7 to 9 minutes or until edges are lightly browned. Let cookies stand on cookie sheets 1 to 2 minutes. Remove cookies with spatula to wire racks; cool completely.

8. To assemble cookies, spread 1 teaspoon jam on flat side of whole cookies, spreading almost to edges. Place cookies with holes, flat-side down, on jam.

9. Store tightly covered at room temperature or freeze up to 3 months.

Makes about 2 dozen cookies

Step 5. Cutting dough with floured cookie cutters.

Step 6. Cutting 1-inch centers out of cookies.

Step 8. Spreading jam on whole cookies.

Viennese Hazelnut Butter Thins

1 cup hazelnuts
1¼ cups powdered sugar
1 cup butter, softened
1 large egg
1 teaspoon vanilla
1¼ cups all-purpose flour
¼ teaspoon salt
1 cup semisweet chocolate chips

1. Preheat oven to 350°F. Spread hazelnuts in single layer on baking sheet. Bake 10 to 12 minutes or until toasted and skins begin to flake off; let cool slightly. Wrap nuts in heavy kitchen towel; rub to remove as much of the skins as possible. Process nuts in food processor until nuts are ground, but not pasty.

2. Beat powdered sugar and butter in medium bowl with electric mixer at medium speed until light and fluffy; scrape bowl once. Beat in egg and vanilla. Gradually add flour and salt. Beat in nuts at low speed until well blended.

3. Place dough on sheet of waxed paper. Roll it back and forth to form a log 12 inches long and 2½ inches wide. Wrap in plastic wrap and refrigerate until firm, 2 hours or up to 48 hours.

4. Preheat oven to 350°F. Cut dough with knife crosswise into ¼-inch-thick slices. Place cookies 2 inches apart on *ungreased* cookie sheets.

5. Bake 10 to 12 minutes or until edges are very lightly browned. Let cookies stand on cookie sheets 1 minute. Remove cookies with spatula to wire racks; cool completely.

6. Melt chocolate chips in 2-cup glass measure in microwave at HIGH 2½ to 3 minutes, stirring once. Dip each cookie into chocolate, coating ½ the way up sides. Let excess chocolate drip back into cup. Transfer cookies to waxed paper; let stand at room temperature 1 hour or until set.

7. Store tightly covered between sheets of waxed paper at room temperature or freeze up to 3 months.   *Makes about 3 dozen cookies*

Step 1. Rubbing hazelnuts gently to remove skins.

Step 3. Rolling dough in waxed paper to form a log.

Step 4. Cutting dough into ¼-inch-thick slices.

Belgian Tuile Cookies

½ cup butter, softened
½ cup sugar
1 large egg white*
1 teaspoon vanilla
¼ teaspoon salt
½ cup all-purpose flour
4 ounces bittersweet chocolate
    candy bar, chopped *or*
    semisweet chocolate chips

*To separate egg, see step 3 on page 46.

1. Preheat oven to 375°F. Grease cookie sheets; set aside.

2. Beat butter and sugar in large bowl with electric mixer at medium speed until light and fluffy, scraping down side of bowl once. Beat in egg white, vanilla and salt. Gradually add flour. Beat at low speed until well blended, scraping down side of bowl once.

3. Drop rounded teaspoonfuls of dough 4 inches apart onto prepared cookie sheets. (Bake only 4 cookies per sheet.) Flatten slightly with spatula.

4. Bake 6 to 8 minutes or until cookies are deep golden brown. Let cookies stand on cookie sheets 1 minute.

5. Working quickly, while cookies are still hot, drape cookies over a rolling pin or bottle so both sides hang down and form a saddle shape; cool completely.

6. Melt chocolate in small, heavy saucepan over low heat, stirring constantly.

7. Tilt saucepan to pool chocolate at one end; dip edge of each cookie into chocolate coating, turning cookie slowly so entire edge is tinged with chocolate.

8. Transfer cookies to waxed paper; let stand at room temperature 1 hour or until set.

9. Store tightly covered at room temperature. Do not freeze.

Makes about 2½ dozen cookies

Step 3. Flattening dough slightly with spatula.

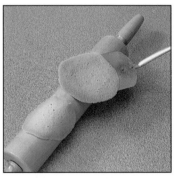

Step 5. Draping cookies over rolling pin.

Step 7. Coating edge of cookie with chocolate.

Bolivian Almond Cookies
(Alfajores de Almendras)

4 cups natural almonds
1 cup all-purpose flour
¼ teaspoon salt
1 cup sugar
¾ cup butter, softened
1 teaspoon vanilla
½ teaspoon almond extract
2 large eggs
2 tablespoons milk
1 tablespoon grated lemon peel
1 cup sliced natural almonds

1. Place whole almonds in food processor. Process using on/off pulsing action until almonds are ground, but not pasty.

2. Preheat oven to 350°F. Grease cookie sheets; set aside.

3. Place ground almonds, flour and salt in medium bowl; stir to combine.

4. Beat sugar, butter, vanilla and almond extract in large bowl with electric mixer at medium speed until light and fluffy, scraping down side of bowl once. Beat in eggs and milk. Gradually add ½ of flour mixture. Beat at low speed until well blended, scraping down side of bowl once. Stir in lemon peel and remaining flour mixture with spoon.

5. Drop rounded teaspoonfuls of dough 2 inches apart onto prepared cookie sheets.

6. Flatten slightly with spoon; top with sliced almonds.

7. Bake 10 to 12 minutes or until edges are lightly browned. Remove cookies with spatula to wire racks; cool completely.

8. Store tightly covered at room temperature or freeze up to 3 months.

Makes about 3 dozen cookies

Step 1. Checking consistency of ground almonds.

Step 5. Dropping rounded teaspoonfuls of dough onto cookie sheet.

Step 6. Topping with sliced almonds.

Czech Bear Paws
(Medvědí Tlapičvky)

4 cups toasted ground hazelnuts*
2 cups all-purpose flour
1 tablespoon unsweetened cocoa
**   powder**
1 teaspoon ground cinnamon
½ teaspoon ground nutmeg
¼ teaspoon salt
1 cup butter, softened
1 cup powdered sugar
1 large egg yolk**
½ cup chocolate chips, melted***
**   Slivered almonds, cut**
**   lengthwise into halves**

*To toast and grind hazelnuts, see step 1 on page 14.

**To separate egg, see step 3 on page 46.

***To melt chocolate, see step 6 on page 76.

1. Preheat oven to 350°F. Place hazelnuts, flour, cocoa, cinnamon, nutmeg and salt in medium bowl; stir to combine.

2. Beat butter, powdered sugar and egg yolk in large bowl with electric mixer at medium speed until light and fluffy, scraping down side of bowl once. Gradually add flour mixture. Beat at low speed until soft dough forms, scraping down side of bowl once.

3. Grease 3 madeleine pans with softened butter, 1 teaspoon per pan; dust with flour. (If only 1 madeleine pan is available, thoroughly wash, dry, regrease and flour after baking each batch. Cover remaining dough with plastic wrap; let stand at room temperature.)

4. Press level tablespoonfuls of dough in each prepared madeleine mold.

5. Bake 12 minutes or until lightly browned. Let cookies stand in pan 3 minutes. Carefully loosen cookies from pan with point of small knife. Invert pan on wire rack. Tap lightly to release cookies; cookies should be shell-side up. Cool completely.

6. Pipe squiggle of melted chocolate on curved end of each cookie; place slivered almond halves on melted chocolate for claws. Let stand at room temperature 1 hour or until set.

7. Store tightly covered at room temperature. These cookies do not freeze well.

Makes about 5 dozen cookies

Step 3. Greasing madeleine pan.

Step 4. Pressing dough in mold.

Step 6. Placing slivered almond halves on chocolate.

Moravian Spice Crisps

⅓ cup shortening
⅓ cup firmly packed brown sugar
¼ cup unsulfured molasses
¼ cup dark corn syrup
1¾ to 2 cups all-purpose flour
2 teaspoons ground ginger
1 teaspoon ground cinnamon
½ teaspoon ground cloves
1¼ teaspoons baking soda
Powdered sugar

1. Melt shortening in small saucepan over low heat. Remove from heat; stir in brown sugar, molasses and corn syrup. Set aside; cool.

2. Combine 1½ cups flour, spices and baking soda in large bowl. Beat in shortening mixture with electric mixer at medium speed; scrape bowl once. Gradually beat in additional flour until stiff dough forms; scrape bowl once.

3. Knead dough on lightly floured surface, adding more flour if too sticky. Form dough into 2 discs; wrap in plastic wrap and refrigerate 30 minutes or until firm.

4. Preheat oven to 350°F. Grease cookie sheets; set aside. Working with 1 disc at a time, unwrap dough and place on lightly floured surface. Roll out dough with lightly floured rolling pin to ¹⁄₁₆-inch thickness.

5. Cut dough with floured 2³⁄₈-inch scalloped cookie cutter. (If dough becomes too soft, refrigerate several minutes before continuing.) Gently press dough trimmings together; reroll and cut out more cookies. (Rerolled dough will produce slightly tougher cookies than first rolling.) Place cookies ½ inch apart on prepared cookie sheets.

6. Bake 8 minutes or until firm and lightly browned. Remove cookies with spatula to wire racks; cool completely.

7. Place small strips of cardboard or parchment paper on cookies; dust with sifted powdered sugar. Carefully remove cardboard. Store tightly covered at room temperature or freeze up to 3 months.

Makes about 6 dozen cookies

Step 1. Stirring brown sugar, molasses and corn syrup.

Step 3. Kneading dough.

Danish Lemon-Filled Spice Cookies (Medaljekager)

Cookies
2¼ cups all-purpose flour
 1 teaspoon ground cinnamon
 ½ teaspoon ground allspice
 ½ teaspoon ground ginger
 ½ teaspoon ground nutmeg
 ¼ teaspoon salt
 1 large egg yolk*
 ¾ cup butter, softened
 ¾ cup granulated sugar
 ¼ cup milk
 1 teaspoon vanilla

Lemon Filling
2¼ cups sifted powdered sugar
1½ tablespoons butter, softened
 3 tablespoons lemon juice
 ½ teaspoon lemon extract

*To separate egg, see step 3 on page 46.

1. For Cookies, place flour, cinnamon, allspice, ginger, nutmeg and salt in medium bowl; stir to combine.

2. Place egg yolk in large bowl; add ¾ cup butter, granulated sugar, milk and vanilla.

3. Beat butter mixture with electric mixer at medium speed until light and fluffy. Gradually add flour mixture. Beat at low speed until dough forms.

4. Form dough into a disc; wrap in plastic wrap and refrigerate 30 minutes or until firm.

5. Preheat oven to 350°F. Grease cookie sheets; set aside.

6. Roll teaspoonfuls of dough into ½-inch balls; place 2 inches apart on prepared cookie sheets. Flatten each ball to ¼-inch thickness with bottom of glass dipped in sugar. Prick top of each cookie using fork.

7. Bake 10 to 13 minutes or until golden brown. Remove cookies with spatula to wire racks; cool completely.

8. For Lemon Filling, beat powdered sugar, 1½ tablespoons butter, lemon juice and lemon extract in medium bowl with electric mixer at medium speed until smooth. Spread filling on flat side of half of cookies. Top with remaining cookies, pressing flat sides together. Let stand at room temperature until set.

9. Store tightly covered at room temperature or freeze up to 3 months.

Makes about 3 dozen sandwiches

Step 2. Adding vanilla.

Step 6. Flattening balls of dough to ¼-inch thickness with glass.

Step 8. Spreading filling on cookies.

Danish Orange Cookies (Orangesmekager)

½ cup butter, softened
¼ cup sugar
1 large egg
½ teaspoon orange extract
2 tablespoons finely grated orange peel
1½ cups all-purpose flour, divided
4 squares (1 ounce each) semisweet chocolate, cut into pieces

1. Beat butter and sugar in large bowl with electric mixer at medium speed until light and fluffy; scrape bowl once. Beat in egg, orange extract and grated peel until well blended; scrape bowl once.

2. Gradually add 1¼ cups flour. Beat at low speed until well blended; scrape bowl occasionally. Stir in remaining ¼ cup flour with spoon to form soft dough. Form dough into a disc; wrap in plastic wrap and refrigerate until firm, 1 hour or overnight.

3. Preheat oven to 400°F. Grease cookie sheets; set aside.

4. On lightly floured surface, roll out dough with lightly floured rolling pin to ¼-inch thickness. Cut dough into 2×1-inch bars. Place bars 2 inches apart on prepared cookie sheets.

5. Gently press dough trimmings together; reroll and cut out more cookies.

6. Bake 10 minutes or until lightly browned. Remove cookies with spatula to wire racks; cool completely.

7. Melt chocolate in 1-cup glass measure in microwave at MEDIUM (50% power) 3 to 4 minutes, stirring twice. Dip one end of each cookie into chocolate, coating ½ the way up sides. Scrape excess chocolate on bottom of cookie back into cup. Transfer cookies to waxed paper; let stand at room temperature 1 hour or until set.

8. Store tightly covered between sheets of waxed paper at room temperature.

Makes about 2½ dozen bars

Step 4. Cutting dough into 2×1-inch bars.

Step 7. Scraping excess chocolate from cookie.

Danish Raspberry Ribbons (Hindbaerkager)

Cookies
  1 cup butter, softened
  ½ cup granulated sugar
  1 large egg
  2 tablespoons milk
  2 tablespoons vanilla
  ¼ teaspoon almond extract
  2 to 2⅔ cups all-purpose flour
  6 tablespoons seedless raspberry
    jam

Glaze
  ½ cup sifted powdered sugar
  1 tablespoon milk
  1 teaspoon vanilla

1. For Cookies, beat butter and granulated sugar in bowl with mixer at medium speed until fluffy; scrape bowl once. Beat in egg, 2 tablespoons milk, 2 tablespoons vanilla and almond extract until blended; scrape bowl once.

2. Gradually add 1½ cups flour. Beat at low speed until well blended; scrape bowl occasionally. Stir in additional flour with spoon until stiff dough forms. Wrap in plastic wrap and refrigerate until firm, 30 minutes or overnight.

3. Preheat oven to 375°F. Cut dough into 6 pieces. Rewrap 3 pieces; refrigerate. With floured hands, shape each dough piece into 12-inch-long, ¾-inch-thick rope.

4. Place ropes 2 inches apart on *ungreased* cookie sheets. Make a ¼-inch-deep groove down center of each rope with handle of wooden spoon. (Ropes flatten to ½-inch-thick strips.)

5. Bake 12 minutes. Spoon 1 tablespoon jam along each groove. Bake 5 to 7 minutes longer or until strips are light golden brown. Cool strips 15 minutes on cookie sheets.

6. For Glaze, place powdered sugar, 1 tablespoon milk and 1 teaspoon vanilla in small bowl; stir until smooth. Drizzle Glaze over strips; let stand 5 minutes to dry. Cut strips at 45° angle into 1-inch slices. Cool cookies completely on wire racks. Repeat with remaining dough.

7. Store tightly covered between sheets of waxed paper at room temperature.
Makes about 5½ dozen cookies

Step 3. Shaping dough into rope.

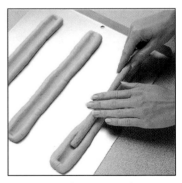
Step 4. Making groove down center of rope.

Danish Cookie Rings (Vanillekranser)

½ cup blanched almonds
2 cups all-purpose flour
¾ cup sugar
¼ teaspoon baking powder
1 cup butter, cut into small pieces
1 large egg
1 tablespoon milk
1 tablespoon vanilla
8 candied red cherries
16 candied green cherries

1. Grease cookie sheets; set aside. Place almonds in food processor. Process using on/off pulsing action until almonds are ground, but not pasty.

2. Place almonds, flour, sugar and baking powder in large bowl; stir to combine. Cut butter into flour mixture with pastry blender or 2 knives until mixture forms pea-sized pieces.

3. Beat egg, milk and vanilla in small bowl with fork until well blended. Add egg mixture to flour mixture; stir with spoon until soft dough forms.

4. Spoon dough into pastry bag fitted with medium star tip. Pipe 3-inch rings 2 inches apart onto prepared cookie sheets. Refrigerate 15 minutes or until firm.

5. Preheat oven to 375°F. Cut cherries into halves. Cut each red cherry half into quarters; cut each green cherry half into 4 slivers.

6. Press red cherry quarter onto each ring where ends meet. Arrange 2 green cherry slivers on either side of red cherry to form leaves.

7. Bake 8 to 10 minutes or until golden. Remove cookies with spatula to wire racks; cool completely.

8. Store tightly covered at room temperature or freeze up to 3 months.

Makes about 5 dozen cookies

Step 4. Piping 3-inch rings onto cookie sheet.

Step 5. Cutting green cherry half into four slivers.

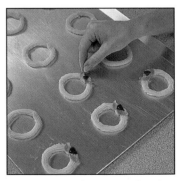
Step 6. Arranging green cherries to form leaves.

English Thumbprint Cookies

1 cup pecan pieces
1¼ cups all-purpose flour
¼ teaspoon salt
½ cup butter, softened
½ cup firmly packed light brown
    sugar
1 teaspoon vanilla
1 large egg, separated*
    Seedless raspberry or
    strawberry jam

*To separate egg, see step 3 on page 46.

1. Preheat oven to 350°F. To toast pecans, spread in single layer on baking sheet. Bake 8 to 10 minutes or until golden brown, stirring frequently. Remove pecans from baking sheet and cool completely.

2. Place pecans in food processor. Process until finely chopped; transfer to shallow bowl.

3. Place flour and salt in medium bowl; stir to combine.

4. Beat butter and brown sugar in large bowl with electric mixer at medium speed until light and fluffy, scraping down side of bowl once. Beat in vanilla and egg yolk. Gradually add flour mixture. Beat at low speed until well blended, scraping down side of bowl once.

5. Beat egg white with fork until frothy.

6. Roll tablespoonfuls of dough into 1-inch balls. Roll balls in egg white; roll in nuts to cover.

7. Place balls 2 inches apart on *ungreased* cookie sheets. Press a deep indentation in center of each ball with thumb.

8. Bake 8 minutes or until set. Fill each indentation with about ¼ teaspoon jam. Bake 8 to 10 minutes longer or until lightly browned. Immediately remove cookies with spatula to wire racks; cool completely.

9. Store tightly covered at room temperature or freeze up to 3 months.

Makes about 2½ dozen cookies

Step 6. Rolling dough balls in nuts.

Step 7. Pressing indentation in centers of dough balls.

Step 8. Filling cookies with jam.

Finnish Spice Cookies (*Nissu Nassu*)

2 cups all-purpose flour
1½ teaspoons ground cinnamon
1½ teaspoons ground ginger
½ teaspoon ground cardamom
½ teaspoon ground cloves
⅔ cup firmly packed light brown sugar
½ cup butter, softened
3 to 5 tablespoons hot water
½ teaspoon baking soda
Royal Icing (page 86)

1. Combine flour and spices in medium bowl.

2. Beat brown sugar and butter in large bowl with electric mixer at medium speed until light and fluffy; scrape bowl once. Place 3 tablespoons water and baking soda in cup; stir until baking soda dissolves. Beat into butter mixture. Gradually add flour mixture. Beat at low speed until dough forms; scrape bowl once. (If dough is too crumbly, add more water, 1 tablespoon at a time, until dough holds together.) Form dough into 2 discs; wrap in plastic wrap and refrigerate until firm, 30 minutes or overnight.

3. Preheat oven to 375°F. Grease cookie sheets; set aside.

4. Working with 1 disc at a time, unwrap dough and place on lightly floured surface. Roll out dough with lightly floured rolling pin to ⅛-inch thickness.

5. Cut dough with floured 3-inch pig-shaped cookie cutter. Place cutouts 1 inch apart on prepared cookie sheets.

6. Gently press dough trimmings together; reroll and cut out more cookies. (Rerolled dough will produce slightly tougher cookies than first rolling.)

7. Bake 8 to 10 minutes or until firm and lightly browned. Remove cookies with spatula to wire racks; cool completely.

8. Prepare Royal Icing. Spoon Icing into pastry bag fitted with writing tip. Decorate cooled cookies with Icing. Let stand at room temperature 1 hour or until set. Store tightly covered at room temperature or freeze up to 3 months. *Makes about 5 dozen cookies*

Step 4. Rolling out dough to ⅛-inch thickness.

Step 5. Cutting dough with floured cookie cutter.

Finnish Nut Logs (Pahkinaleivat)

1 cup butter, softened
½ cup plus ⅓ cup sugar, divided
3 large eggs, divided
½ teaspoon ground cardamom
½ teaspoon almond extract
2¼ to 2½ cups all-purpose flour
1 cup finely chopped almonds*

*To chop almonds, see step 3 on page 40.

1. Beat butter and ½ cup sugar in large bowl with electric mixer at medium speed until light and fluffy, scraping down side of bowl once. Beat in 1 egg, cardamom and almond extract until well mixed, scraping down side of bowl once.

2. Gradually add 1½ cups flour. Beat at low speed until well blended, scraping down side of bowl occasionally. Stir in additional flour with spoon until soft dough forms. Form dough into a disc; wrap in plastic wrap and refrigerate until firm, 30 minutes or overnight.

3. Grease cookie sheets; set aside. Cut dough into 8 equal pieces.

4. With floured hands, shape each piece of dough into 12-inch-long, ½-inch-thick rope. Cut ropes into 2-inch logs. Place logs on prepared cookie sheets; refrigerate 30 minutes.

5. Preheat oven to 350°F. Beat remaining 2 eggs in shallow dish with fork until foamy.

6. Place almonds and ⅓ cup sugar in medium bowl; stir to combine. Dip logs into beaten egg mixture; roll in nut mixture to cover.

7. Place logs 2 inches apart on prepared cookie sheets. Bake 15 minutes or until lightly browned. Remove cookies with spatula to wire racks; cool completely.

8. Store tightly covered at room temperature or freeze up to 3 months.

Makes about 4 dozen cookies

Step 3. Cutting dough into eight equal pieces.

Step 5. Beating eggs until foamy.

Step 6. Rolling dough logs in nut mixture.

Chocolate Madeleines

1¼ cups cake flour or all-purpose
     flour
¼ cup unsweetened cocoa powder
¼ teaspoon salt
¼ teaspoon baking powder
1 cup granulated sugar
2 large eggs
¾ cup butter, melted and cooled
2 tablespoons almond-flavored
     liqueur or kirsch
     Powdered sugar

1. Preheat oven to 375°F. Grease 3 madeleine pans with softened butter, 1 teaspoon per pan; dust with flour; set aside. (If only 1 madeleine pan is available, thoroughly wash, dry, regrease and flour after baking each batch. Cover remaining dough with plastic wrap; let stand at room temperature.)

2. Place flour, cocoa, salt and baking powder in medium bowl; stir to combine.

3. Beat granulated sugar and eggs in large bowl with electric mixer at medium speed 5 minutes or until mixture is light in color, thick and falls in wide ribbons from beaters, scraping down side of bowl once.

4. Beat in flour mixture at low speed until well blended, scraping down side of bowl once. Beat in melted butter and liqueur until just blended.

5. Spoon level tablespoonfuls of batter into each prepared madeleine mold. Bake 12 minutes or until puffed and golden brown.

6. Let cookies stand in pan 1 minute. Carefully loosen cookies from pan with point of small knife. Invert pan on wire rack. Tap lightly to release cookies; cookies should be shell-side up. Cool completely.

7. Dust with sifted powdered sugar.

8. Store tightly covered at room temperature up to 24 hours or freeze up to 3 months.
Makes about 2 dozen madeleines

Step 1. Greasing madeleine pan.

Step 5. Spooning tablespoonfuls of batter into madeleine mold.

Step 7. Dusting with powdered sugar.

Orange-Almond Sables

¾ **cup whole blanched almonds**
1½ **cups powdered sugar**
1 **cup butter, softened**
1 **tablespoon finely grated orange peel**
1 **tablespoon almond-flavored liqueur** *or* **1 teaspoon almond extract**
1¾ **cups all-purpose flour**
¼ **teaspoon salt**
1 **large egg, beaten**

1. Preheat oven to 375°F. To toast almonds, spread in single layer on baking sheet. Bake 8 to 10 minutes or until golden brown, stirring frequently. Remove almonds from baking sheet and cool; set aside.

2. Beat powdered sugar and butter in large bowl with electric mixer at medium speed until light and fluffy, scraping down side of bowl once. Beat in orange peel and liqueur.

3. Set aside 24 whole almonds. Place remaining cooled almonds in food processor. Process using on/off pulsing action until almonds are ground, but not pasty.

4. Place ground almonds, flour and salt in medium bowl; stir to combine. Gradually add to butter mixture. Beat with electric mixer at low speed until well blended, scraping down side of bowl once.

5. Place dough on lightly floured surface. Roll out dough with lightly floured rolling pin to just under ¼-inch thickness. Cut dough with floured 2½-inch fluted or round cookie cutter. Place cookies 2 inches apart on *ungreased* cookie sheets.

6. Lightly brush tops of cookies with beaten egg. Press one whole reserved almond in center of each cookie.

7. Brush almonds lightly with beaten egg. Bake 10 to 12 minutes or until light golden brown.

8. Let cookies stand 1 minute on cookie sheets. Remove cookies with spatula to wire racks; cool completely. Store tightly covered at room temperature or freeze up to 3 months.

Makes about 2 dozen cookies

Step 5. Cutting dough with floured cookie cutter.

Step 6. Pressing whole almond in center of cookie.

Step 7. Brushing almond with beaten egg.

Pfeffernüsse

3½ cups all-purpose flour
2 teaspoons baking powder
1½ teaspoons ground cinnamon
1 teaspoon ground ginger
½ teaspoon baking soda
½ teaspoon salt
½ teaspoon ground cloves
½ teaspoon ground cardamom
¼ teaspoon freshly ground black
   pepper
1 cup butter, softened
1 cup granulated sugar
¼ cup dark molasses
1 large egg
   Powdered sugar

1. Place flour, baking powder, cinnamon, ginger, baking soda, salt, cloves, cardamom and pepper in large bowl; stir to combine.

2. Beat butter and granulated sugar in large bowl with electric mixer at medium speed until light and fluffy, scraping down side of bowl once. Beat in molasses and egg. Gradually add flour mixture. Beat at low speed until dough forms, scraping down side of bowl once. Form dough into a disc; wrap in plastic wrap and refrigerate until firm, 30 minutes or up to 3 days.

3. Preheat oven to 350°F. Grease cookie sheets; set aside.

4. Roll dough into 1-inch balls; place 2 inches apart on prepared cookie sheets. Bake 12 to 14 minutes or until golden brown.

5. Remove cookies with spatula to wire racks; dust with sifted powdered sugar. Cool completely.

6. Store tightly covered at room temperature or freeze up to 3 months.

Makes about 5 dozen cookies

Step 2. Beating molasses and egg into butter mixture.

Step 4. Rolling dough into 1-inch balls.

Step 5. Dusting with powdered sugar.

German Honey Bars (Lebkuchen)

2¾ cups all-purpose flour
2 teaspoons ground cinnamon
1 teaspoon baking powder
½ teaspoon baking soda
½ teaspoon salt
½ teaspoon ground cardamom
½ teaspoon ground ginger
½ cup honey
½ cup dark molasses
¾ cup firmly packed brown sugar
3 tablespoons butter, melted
1 large egg
½ cup chopped toasted almonds
    (optional)
Glaze (recipe follows)

1. Preheat oven to 350°F. Grease 15×10-inch jelly-roll pan; set aside.

2. Place flour, cinnamon, baking powder, baking soda, salt, cardamom and ginger in medium bowl; stir to combine.

3. Combine honey and molasses in medium saucepan; bring to a boil over medium heat. Remove from heat; cool 10 minutes.

4. Stir brown sugar, butter and egg into honey mixture.

5. Place brown sugar mixture in large bowl. Gradually add flour mixture. Beat at low speed with electric mixer until dough forms, scraping down side of bowl once. Stir in almonds with spoon. (Dough will be slightly sticky.)

6. Spread dough evenly into prepared pan. Bake 20 to 22 minutes or until golden brown and set. Remove pan to wire rack; cool completely.

7. Prepare Glaze. Spread over cooled cookie. Let stand until set, about 30 minutes. Cut into 2×1-inch bars.

8. Store tightly covered at room temperature or freeze up to 3 months.

Makes about 6 dozen bars

Glaze

1¼ cups sifted powdered sugar
3 tablespoons fresh lemon juice
1 teaspoon grated lemon peel

Place all ingredients in medium bowl; stir with spoon until smooth.

Step 3. Bringing honey mixture to a boil.

Step 4. Stirring in brown sugar, butter and egg.

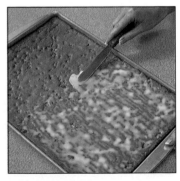
Step 7. Spreading Glaze over cooled cookie.

Greek Lemon-Herb Cookies

2 lemons
2½ cups all-purpose flour
1 teaspoon baking soda
¼ teaspoon salt
2 large eggs
1 cup butter, softened
1¼ cups sugar, divided
½ teaspoon dried rosemary leaves,
    crushed

1. Finely grate colored portion of lemon peel using bell grater or hand-held grater. Measure 4 teaspoons; set aside.

2. Preheat oven to 375°F. Place flour, baking soda and salt in large bowl; stir to combine.

3. To separate egg yolk from white, gently tap egg in center against hard surface, such as side of bowl. Holding a shell half in each hand, gently transfer yolk back and forth between the 2 halves. Allow white to drip down the 2 halves into bowl. When all white has dripped into bowl, place yolk in another bowl. Store unused egg whites in airtight container. Refrigerate for up to one week.

4. Beat butter and 1 cup sugar in large bowl with electric mixer at medium speed until light and fluffy; scrape bowl once. Beat in egg yolks, 3 teaspoons lemon peel and rosemary.

5. Gradually add flour mixture. Beat at low speed until well blended; scrape bowl once.

6. Combine remaining ¼ cup sugar and 1 teaspoon lemon peel in small bowl.

7. Roll tablespoonfuls of dough into 1-inch balls. Roll balls in sugar mixture to coat.

8. Place balls 2 inches apart on *ungreased* cookie sheets. Flatten each ball to ¼-inch thickness with bottom of glass.

9. Bake 10 to 12 minutes or until edges are golden brown. Remove cookies with spatula to wire racks; cool completely.

10. Store tightly covered at room temperature or freeze up to 3 months.

Makes about 4 dozen cookies

Step 3. Separating an egg.

Step 7. Rolling dough balls in sugar mixture.

Step 8. Flattening dough balls to ¼-inch thickness with glass.

Dutch Chocolate Meringues

¼ **cup finely chopped pecans***
2½ **tablespoons unsweetened cocoa**
    powder (preferably Dutch
    process)
  3 **large egg whites****
¼ **teaspoon salt**
¾ **cup granulated sugar**
    Powdered sugar (optional)

*To chop pecans, see step 1 on page 50.

**To separate eggs, see step 3 on page 46.

1. Preheat oven to 200°F. Line cookie sheets with foil; grease well. Set aside.

2. Place pecans and cocoa in medium bowl; stir to combine.

3. Beat egg whites and salt in clean large bowl with electric mixer at high speed until light and foamy. Gradually beat in granulated sugar until stiff peaks form.

4. Gently fold in pecan mixture with rubber spatula by gently cutting down to the bottom of the bowl, scraping up the side of the bowl, then folding over the top of the mixture. Repeat until pecan mixture is evenly incorporated into egg white mixture.

5. Spoon dough into pastry bag fitted with large plain tip. Pipe 1-inch mounds 2 inches apart onto prepared cookie sheets. Bake 1 hour. Turn oven off. Do not open oven door; let stand in oven until set, 2 hours or overnight.

6. When cookies are firm, carefully peel cookies from foil. Dust with powdered sugar.

7. Store loosely covered at room temperature up to 2 days. *Makes about 6 dozen cookies*

Meringue Mushrooms: Pipe same number of 1-inch-tall "stems" as mounds. Bake as directed in step 5. When cookies are firm, attach "stems" to "caps" with melted chocolate.*** Dust with sifted unsweetened cocoa powder.

***To melt chocolate, see step 6 on page 76.

Step 3. Checking for stiff peaks.

Step 4. Folding pecan mixture into egg white mixture.

Step 5. Piping 1-inch mounds onto cookie sheet.

Mexican Wedding Cookies

1 cup pecan pieces or halves
1 cup unsalted butter, softened
2 cups powdered sugar, divided
2 cups all-purpose flour, divided
2 teaspoons vanilla
¼ teaspoon salt

1. Place pecans in food processor. Process using on/off pulsing action until pecans are ground, but not pasty.

2. Beat butter and ½ cup powdered sugar in large bowl with electric mixer at medium speed until light and fluffy, scraping down side of bowl once. Gradually add 1 cup flour, vanilla and salt. Beat at low speed until well blended, scraping down side of bowl once. Stir in remaining flour and ground nuts with spoon.

3. Form dough into a ball; wrap in plastic wrap and refrigerate 1 hour or until firm.

4. Preheat oven to 350°F. Roll tablespoonfuls of dough into 1-inch balls; place 1 inch apart on *ungreased* cookie sheets.

5. Bake 12 to 15 minutes or until pale golden brown. Let cookies stand on cookie sheets 2 minutes.

6. Meanwhile, place 1 cup powdered sugar in 13×9-inch glass dish. Transfer hot cookies to dish.

7. Roll cookies in powdered sugar, coating well. Let cookies cool in sugar.

8. Sift remaining ½ cup powdered sugar over sugar-coated cookies before serving.

9. Store tightly covered at room temperature or freeze up to 1 month.

Makes about 4 dozen cookies

Step 3. Forming dough into a ball.

Step 6. Placing hot cookies in powdered sugar.

Step 7. Rolling cookies in powdered sugar.

Mexican Sugar Cookies (Polvorones)

1 cup butter, softened
½ cup powdered sugar
2 tablespoons milk
1 teaspoon vanilla
1 teaspoon ground cinnamon, divided
1½ to 1¾ cups all-purpose flour
1 teaspoon baking powder
1 cup granulated sugar
1 square (1 ounce) semisweet chocolate, finely grated

1. Preheat oven to 325°F. Grease cookie sheets; set aside.

2. Beat butter, powdered sugar, milk, vanilla and ½ teaspoon cinnamon in large bowl with electric mixer at medium speed until light and fluffy, scraping down side of bowl once. Gradually add 1½ cups flour and baking powder. Beat at low speed until well blended, scraping down side of bowl once. Stir in additional flour with spoon if dough is too soft to shape.

3. Roll tablespoonfuls of dough into 1¼-inch balls; place 3 inches apart on prepared cookie sheets. Flatten each ball into 2-inch round with bottom of glass dipped in granulated sugar.

4. Bake 20 to 25 minutes or until edges are golden brown. Let stand on cookie sheets 3 to 4 minutes.

5. Meanwhile, combine granulated sugar, grated chocolate and remaining ½ teaspoon cinnamon in small bowl; stir to combine. Transfer cookies, one at a time, with spatula to sugar mixture; coat on both sides. Remove with spatula to wire racks; cool completely.

6. Store tightly covered at room temperature or freeze up to 3 months.

Makes about 2 dozen cookies

Step 2. Stirring in additional flour.

Step 3. Placing dough balls 3 inches apart on cookie sheet.

Step 5. Coating cookies with sugar mixture.

Norwegian Pepper Cookies (Pepperkaker)

Cookies
    4 to 4½ cups all-purpose flour,
        divided
    1 teaspoon baking soda
    1 teaspoon ground cardamom
    1 teaspoon ground cinnamon
    1 teaspoon ground cloves
    ½ teaspoon ground black pepper
    ½ teaspoon salt
    ½ cup butter, softened
2½ cups powdered sugar, divided
    4 large eggs
    3 tablespoons lemon juice
    1 tablespoon grated lemon peel*
    ½ teaspoon almond extract
    ½ cup diced candied citron, finely
        chopped

Lemon Glaze
    2 cups sifted powdered sugar
    3 to 4 tablespoons lemon juice

*To grate lemon peel, see step 1 on
page 78.

1. For Cookies, place 4 cups flour, baking soda, cardamom, cinnamon, cloves, pepper and salt in medium bowl; stir to combine. Beat butter and 1¼ cups powdered sugar in large bowl with electric mixer at medium speed until light and fluffy, scraping down side of bowl once. Beat in eggs and remaining 1¼ cups powdered sugar, scraping down side of bowl once.

2. Gradually add flour mixture. Beat at low speed until well blended, scraping down side of bowl once. Beat in 3 tablespoons lemon juice, lemon peel and almond extract. Stir in citron and remaining flour with spoon until stiff dough forms.

3. Roll tablespoonfuls of dough into 1-inch balls; place on large baking sheet or tray. Cover with plastic wrap and refrigerate until firm, 2 hours or overnight.

4. Preheat oven to 350°F. Grease cookie sheets. Place balls 1 inch apart on prepared cookie sheets. Bake 13 to 15 minutes or until firm and light golden brown. Remove cookies with spatula to wire racks.

5. For Lemon Glaze, place 2 cups powdered sugar and 3 tablespoons lemon juice in large bowl. Stir until smooth and spreadable. If mixture is too stiff, add more lemon juice. While still warm, brush cookies with Lemon Glaze. Let stand at room temperature 1 hour or until set.

6. Store tightly covered at room temperature or freeze up to 3 months.

Makes about 7 dozen cookies

Step 2. Stirring in citron and remaining flour.

Step 5. Brushing cookies with Lemon Glaze.

Norwegian Wreaths (Berliner Kranser)

1 hard-cooked large egg yolk
1 large egg, separated*
½ cup butter, softened
½ cup powdered sugar
½ teaspoon vanilla
1¼ cups all-purpose flour, divided
    Coarse sugar crystals or
      crushed sugar cubes

*To separate egg, see step 3 on page 46.

1. Preheat oven to 350°F. Grease cookie sheets; set aside.

2. Beat cooked and raw egg yolks in medium bowl with electric mixer at medium speed until smooth.

3. Beat in butter, powdered sugar and vanilla, scraping down side of bowl once. Stir in 1 cup flour with spoon. Stir in remaining flour until stiff dough forms.

4. Place dough on sheet of waxed paper. Using waxed paper to hold dough, roll it back and forth to form a log; cut log into 18 equal pieces. Roll each piece of dough into an 8-inch rope, tapering ends.

5. Shape ropes into wreaths; overlap ends and let extend out from wreath.

6. Place wreaths on prepared cookie sheets. Refrigerate 15 minutes or until firm.

7. Beat reserved egg white with fork until foamy. Brush wreaths with egg white; sprinkle with sugar crystals. Bake 8 to 10 minutes or until light golden brown. Remove cookies with spatula to wire racks; cool completely.

8. Store tightly covered at room temperature or freeze up to 3 months.

Makes about 1½ dozen cookies

Step 2. Beating egg yolks until smooth.

Step 4. Rolling dough into 8-inch ropes.

Step 5. Shaping ropes into wreaths.

Polish Fried Cookies (Chrusciki)

1 cup all-purpose flour
1 tablespoon granulated sugar
3 large egg yolks*
3 tablespoons sour cream
1 tablespoon vodka or whiskey
Vegetable oil for frying
2⅔ cups powdered sugar

*To separate eggs, see step 3 on page 46.

1. Place flour and granulated sugar in medium bowl; stir to combine. Make well in center of flour mixture; add egg yolks, sour cream and vodka. Stir with spoon until soft dough forms.

2. Place dough on lightly floured surface; knead gently until dough is smooth. Form dough into 2 discs; wrap in plastic wrap and refrigerate until firm, 30 minutes or overnight.

3. Working with 1 disc at a time, unwrap dough and place on lightly floured surface. Roll out dough with lightly floured rolling pin to ⅛-inch-thick, 12×10-inch rectangle. Cut dough lengthwise in half; cut each half into 12 strips.

4. Make 1-inch vertical slit down center of each strip. Insert one end of strip through slit to form twist; repeat with each strip.

5. Heat oil in large saucepan to 375°F. Place 6 strips at a time in hot oil.

6. Fry about 1 minute or until golden brown, turning cookies once with slotted spoon. Drain on paper towels.

7. Place ⅓ cup powdered sugar in small brown paper bag. Add 6 warm cookies at a time; close bag and shake until cookies are coated with sugar. Repeat with additional sugar and remaining cookies.

8. Cookies are best when served immediately, but can be stored in an airtight container 1 day.
Makes 4 dozen cookies

Step 5. Placing dough strips in hot oil.

Step 6. Turning cookies with slotted spoon.

Step 7. Shaking cookies in powdered sugar.

Polish Honey Bars (Piernikowa Krajanka Swiateczna)

½ **cup granulated sugar, divided**
2 **tablespoons boiling water**
⅓ **cup honey**
2 **tablespoons margarine**
1 **teaspoon ground allspice**
½ **teaspoon ground cinnamon**
¼ **teaspoon ground cloves**
¼ **teaspoon ground nutmeg**
2 **cups all-purpose flour**
3 **tablespoons cold water**
1 **large egg**
1 **teaspoon baking soda**
   Chocolate Filling (page 62)
1 **cup semisweet chocolate chips**
32 **whole toasted almonds***

*To toast almonds, see step 1 on page 40.

1. Combine 2 tablespoons granulated sugar and boiling water in small heavy saucepan over medium heat; stir until sugar dissolves and is slightly brown. Add remaining granulated sugar, honey, margarine, allspice, cinnamon, cloves and nutmeg; bring to a boil over high heat, stirring constantly. Remove from heat; pour mixture into medium bowl. Cool.

2. Add flour, cold water, egg and baking soda to cooled sugar mixture; stir with spoon until well blended. Cover; let stand 20 minutes.

3. Preheat oven to 350°F. Grease and flour 15×10-inch jelly-roll pan; set aside. Roll out dough on lightly floured surface with lightly floured rolling pin to almost fit size of pan.

4. Press dough evenly into pan to edges. Bake 10 to 13 minutes or until dough springs back when lightly touched in center. Remove pan to wire rack; cool completely.

5. To remove cookie base from pan, run knife around edge of cookie base to loosen it from sides of pan. Place wire rack top-side down over pan; flip rack and pan over together. Cookie base should drop out of pan onto rack.

6. Cut cookie base in half to form two rectangles.

continued on page 62

Step 4. Pressing dough into pan.

Step 5. Running knife around edge of pan to loosen cookie.

Step 6. Cutting cookie base in half.

Polish Honey Bars, continued

7. Prepare Chocolate Filling; spread evenly over 1 rectangle. Top with other rectangle, flat-side up. Wrap cookie sandwich in plastic wrap.

8. Place baking sheet on top of cookie sandwich; place heavy cans or other weights on baking sheet to press sandwich layers together. Let cookie sandwich stand overnight.

9. When cookie is ready to frost, melt 1 cup chocolate chips in 2-cup glass measure in microwave at MEDIUM (50% power) 3 to 4 minutes, stirring occasionally. Dip wide part of each whole almond into chocolate; place dipped almonds on waxed paper to set.

10. Remove weights and baking sheet from cookie sandwich; unwrap. Spread remaining melted chocolate over top. Before chocolate sets, score top of cookie sandwich into 32 bars.

11. Place 1 dipped almond on each bar. (If chocolate has set, it may be necessary to reheat almonds in microwave for a few seconds.) Let stand at room temperature until set; cut into bars.

12. Store tightly covered at room temperature or freeze up to 3 months.
Makes 32 bars

Chocolate Filling

¼ cup whipping cream
½ cup semisweet chocolate chips
 1 cup natural almonds, toasted and
    ground*
½ to ¾ cup sifted powdered sugar
½ teaspoon vanilla

*To toast almonds, see step 1 on page 40. To grind almonds, see step 1 on page 18.

Heat cream and ¹⁄₂ cup chocolate chips in small saucepan over medium heat until melted and smooth, stirring constantly. Remove from heat; stir in ground almonds, ¹⁄₂ cup powdered sugar and vanilla with spoon. Stir in additional powdered sugar until stiff enough to spread.
Makes about 1 cup filling

Step 7. Spreading Chocolate Filling over one rectangle.

Step 8. Placing heavy cans on baking sheet to press cookie sandwich layers together.

Step 10. Scoring top of cookie sandwich into bars.

Georgian Baklava (Pakhlava)

2 cups all-purpose flour
½ teaspoon baking soda
1 cup butter, cut into pieces
2 large eggs, separated*
½ cup sour cream
1 cup finely ground walnuts**
1 cup dried fruit bits
¾ cup sugar
½ teaspoon ground cinnamon
2 teaspoons water

*To separate eggs, see step 3 on page 46.

**To grind walnuts, see information on grinding almonds, step 1 on page 18.

1. Place flour and baking soda in large bowl; stir to combine. Cut butter into flour mixture with pastry blender or 2 knives until mixture forms pea-sized pieces.

2. Reserve 1 egg yolk in cup; cover with plastic wrap. Add remaining yolk and sour cream to flour mixture; toss with fork until mixture holds together. Form dough into a ball; wrap in plastic wrap and refrigerate 2 hours or until firm.

3. Meanwhile, for filling, combine walnuts, dried fruit, sugar and cinnamon in medium bowl; set aside. Beat egg whites in clean large bowl with electric mixer at high speed until stiff peaks form. (After beaters are lifted from egg whites, stiff peaks should remain on surface, and when bowl is tilted, mixture should not slide around.)

4. Gently fold in fruit mixture with rubber spatula by gently cutting down to the bottom of the bowl, scraping up the side of the bowl, then folding over the top of the mixture. Repeat until fruit mixture is evenly incorporated into the egg whites.

continued on page 64

Step 1. Cutting butter into flour mixture to form pea-sized pieces.

Step 3. Checking for stiff peaks.

Step 4. Folding fruit mixture into egg whites.

5. Grease and lightly flour 9-inch square baking pan. Divide dough into 3 equal pieces. Shape each piece into a 3-inch square about 1 inch thick. Place each square between two pieces of well-floured waxed paper. Roll each piece into a 9-inch square. (You may have to lift paper and dust dough with flour occasionally to prevent sticking.)

6. Remove top sheet of waxed paper from 1 dough square. Invert dough in bottom of baking pan. (You may have to trim dough to fit pan.) Remove second sheet of waxed paper.

7. Add water to reserved egg yolk; beat lightly with fork until foamy. Brush dough with egg yolk mixture. Spread half of fruit mixture on dough. Repeat procedure with second dough square, egg yolk mixture and remaining fruit mixture. Cover with third dough square; turn edges under for neat appearance.

8. Preheat oven to 350°F. Score top of dough into diamonds by making lengthwise diagonal cuts, just through top layers of dough, every 1½ inches, with sharp knife. Make crosswise horizontal cuts, just through top layers of dough, to form diamond shapes.

9. Brush dough with remaining egg yolk mixture. Bake 45 minutes or until browned. Remove pan to wire rack; cool completely. Cut bars all the way through with serrated knife; carefully lift bars out of pan with thin flexible spatula.

10. Store tightly covered in single layer.

Makes about 2½ dozen bars

Step 5. Placing 3-inch square between two pieces of waxed paper.

Step 6. Removing top sheet of waxed paper.

Step 8. Scoring layers of dough to form diamond shapes.

Molded Scotch Shortbread

1½ cups all-purpose flour
¼ teaspoon salt
¾ cup butter, softened
⅓ cup sugar
1 large egg
   10-inch round ceramic
     shortbread mold

1. Preheat oven to temperature recommended by shortbread mold manufacturer. Place flour and salt in medium bowl; stir to combine.

2. Beat butter and sugar in large bowl with electric mixer at medium speed until light and fluffy, scraping down side of bowl once.

3. Beat in egg. Gradually add flour mixture. Beat at low speed until well blended, scraping down side of bowl once.

4. Spray shortbread mold with nonstick cooking spray. Press dough firmly in mold. Bake, cool and remove from mold according to manufacturer's directions.

5. If mold is not available, preheat oven to 350°F. Roll tablespoonfuls of dough into 1-inch balls; place 2 inches apart on *ungreased* cookie sheets. Press with fork to flatten.

6. Bake 18 to 20 minutes or until edges are lightly browned. Let cookies stand on cookie sheets 2 minutes. Remove cookies with spatula to wire racks; cool completely.

7. Store tightly covered at room temperature or freeze up to 3 months.

Makes 1 shortbread mold or 2 dozen cookies

Step 2. Scraping butter mixture from side of bowl.

Step 4. Pressing dough in mold.

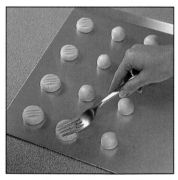
Step 5. Pressing dough balls with fork to flatten.

Churros

1 cup water
¼ cup butter or margarine
6 tablespoons sugar, divided
¼ teaspoon salt
1 cup all-purpose flour
2 large eggs
  Vegetable oil for frying
1 teaspoon ground cinnamon

1. Place water, butter, 2 tablespoons sugar and salt in medium saucepan; bring to a boil over high heat.

2. Remove from heat; add flour. Beat with spoon until dough forms ball and releases from side of pan.

3. Vigorously beat in eggs, 1 at a time, until mixture is smooth.

4. Spoon dough into pastry bag fitted with large star tip.

5. Pipe 3×1-inch strips onto baking sheet lined with waxed paper. Place baking sheet in freezer; freeze 20 minutes.

6. Pour oil into 10-inch skillet to ¾-inch depth. Heat oil to 375°F. Place 4 or 5 cookies at a time into hot oil. Fry 3 to 4 minutes or until deep golden brown, turning cookies once with spatula. Drain on paper towels.

7. Combine remaining 4 tablespoons sugar with cinnamon. Place in small brown paper bag. Add warm cookies 1 at a time; close bag and shake until cookie is coated with sugar mixture. Repeat with additional sugar mixture and remaining cookies.

8. Cookies are best when served immediately, but can be stored in an airtight container 1 day.

Makes about 3 dozen cookies

Step 3. Beating eggs into dough.

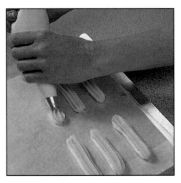
Step 5. Piping 3×1-inch strips onto baking sheet.

Step 6. Turning cookies with spatula.

Swedish Sandwich Cookies (Syltkakor)

1 cup butter, softened
½ cup plus 2 tablespoons sugar,
   divided
1 large egg yolk*
1 large egg, separated*
2 to 2¼ cups all-purpose flour
3 tablespoons ground almonds**
   Red currant or strawberry jelly

*To separate eggs, see step 3 on page 46.

**To grind almonds, see step 1 on page 18.

1. Beat butter and ½ cup sugar in large bowl with mixer at medium speed until fluffy; scrape bowl once. Beat in egg yolks; scrape bowl once. Add 1½ cups flour; beat at low speed until well blended. Stir in additional flour with spoon until stiff dough forms. Divide dough in half. Refrigerate, covered, until firm, at least 2 hours.

2. Preheat oven to 375°F. Grease and flour cookie sheets; set aside. Roll out 1 piece of dough on lightly floured surface with lightly floured rolling pin to ³⁄₁₆-inch thickness. Cut dough with floured 2¼-inch round cookie cutter. Place cookies 1½ inches apart on prepared cookie sheets. Gently press dough trimmings together; reroll and cut out more cookies.

3. Roll out second piece of dough as step 2 directs. Cut dough with floured 2¼-inch scalloped cookie cutter. Cut 1-inch centers out of scalloped cookies. Place cookies 1½ inches apart on prepared cookie sheets. Cut equal numbers of round and scalloped cookies.

4. Beat egg white in small cup with wire whisk. Place almonds and remaining 2 tablespoons sugar in small bowl; stir to combine. Brush each scalloped cookie with egg white; sprinkle with almond mixture. Bake cookies 8 to 10 minutes or until firm and light golden brown. Remove cookies to wire racks; cool completely.

5. To assemble cookies, spread about ½ teaspoon currant jelly on flat side of round cookies; top with flat side of scalloped cookies. Store tightly covered at room temperature or freeze up to 3 months.
Makes 1½ dozen sandwich cookies

Step 3. Cutting 1-inch centers out of scalloped cookies.

Step 4. Brushing scalloped cookies with egg whites.

Step 5. Spreading jelly on round cookies.

Christmas Spritz Cookies

2¼ cups all-purpose flour
¼ teaspoon salt
1¼ cups powdered sugar
1 cup butter, softened
1 large egg
1 teaspoon vanilla
1 teaspoon almond extract
  Green food coloring (optional)
  Candied red and green cherries
    and assorted decorative
    candies, as desired

1. Preheat oven to 375°F. Place flour and salt in medium bowl; stir to combine.

2. Beat powdered sugar and butter in large bowl with electric mixer at medium speed until light and fluffy, scraping down side of bowl once. Beat in egg, vanilla and almond extract. Gradually add flour mixture. Beat at low speed until well blended, scraping down side of bowl once.

3. Divide dough in half. Tint half the dough green with food coloring.

4. Fit cookie press with desired plate (or change plates for different shapes after first batch). Fill press with dough; press dough 1 inch apart on *ungreased* cookie sheets.

5. Decorate with cherries and assorted candies.

6. Bake 10 to 12 minutes or until just set. Remove cookies with spatula to wire racks; cool completely.

7. Store tightly covered at room temperature or freeze up to 3 months.

Makes about 5 dozen cookies

Step 3. Tinting dough green with food coloring.

Step 4. Filling cookie press with dough.

Step 5. Decorating cookies.

Swedish Cookie Shells (Sandbakelser)

1 cup butter, softened
⅔ cup sugar
1 large egg white*
1 teaspoon vanilla
½ teaspoon almond extract
2 cups all-purpose flour, divided
¼ cup finely ground blanched
   almonds**

*To separate egg, see step 3 on page 46.

**To grind almonds, see step 1 on page 18.

1. Beat butter and sugar in large bowl with electric mixer at medium speed until light and fluffy, scraping down side of bowl once. Beat in egg white, vanilla and almond extract until well blended, scraping down side of bowl once.

2. Gradually add 1½ cups flour and almonds. Beat at low speed until well blended, scraping down side of bowl once. Stir in remaining flour with spoon until soft dough forms. Form dough into 1-inch-thick square; wrap in plastic wrap and refrigerate until firm, 1 hour or overnight.

3. Preheat oven to 375°F. Press rounded teaspoonfuls of dough in greased sandbakelser tins or mini muffin pan cups.

4. Place tins on baking sheet. Bake 8 to 10 minutes or until cookie shells are lightly browned. Cool cookies in tins 1 minute.

5. Carefully loosen cookies from tins with point of small knife. Invert tins on wire racks. Tap lightly to release cookies; cookies should be shell-side up. Cool completely. Repeat with remaining dough; cool cookie tins between batches.

6. Serve cookies shell-side up. Store tightly covered at room temperature or freeze up to 3 months.   *Makes about 10 dozen cookies*

Step 3. Pressing dough in sandbakelser tins.

Step 5. Loosening cookies from tins.

Swiss Mocha Treats

2 ounces imported Swiss
    bittersweet chocolate candy
    bar, broken
½ cup plus 2 tablespoons butter,
    softened, divided
1 tablespoon instant espresso
    powder
1 teaspoon vanilla
1¾ cups all-purpose flour
½ teaspoon baking soda
½ teaspoon salt
¾ cup sugar
1 large egg
3 ounces imported Swiss white
    chocolate candy bar, broken

1. Melt bittersweet chocolate and 2 tablespoons butter in small, heavy saucepan over low heat, stirring often. Add espresso powder; stir until dissolved. Remove from heat; stir in vanilla. Let cool to room temperature.

2. Place flour, baking soda and salt in medium bowl; stir to combine.

3. Beat ½ cup butter and sugar in large bowl with mixer at medium speed until fluffy; scrape bowl once. Beat in bittersweet chocolate mixture and egg. Gradually add flour mixture. Beat at low speed until well blended; scrape bowl once. Cover; refrigerate 30 minutes or until firm.

4. Preheat oven to 375°F. Roll tablespoonfuls of dough into 1-inch balls; place 3 inches apart on *ungreased* cookie sheets. Flatten each ball into ½-inch-thick round with fork dipped in sugar.

5. Bake 9 to 10 minutes or until set (do not overbake or cookies will become dry). Immediately remove cookies with spatula to wire racks; cool completely.

6. Place white chocolate in small resealable plastic freezer bag; seal bag. Microwave at MEDIUM (50% power) 1 minute. Turn bag over; microwave at MEDIUM 1 minute or until melted. Knead until chocolate is smooth.

7. Cut off tiny corner of bag; pipe or drizzle white chocolate onto cooled cookies. Let stand 30 minutes or until set.

8. Store tightly covered at room temperature or freeze up to 3 months.

Makes about 4 dozen cookies

Step 4. Rolling dough into 1-inch balls.

Step 6. Kneading bag until chocolate is smooth.

Step 7. Drizzling white chocolate onto cooled cookies.

Luscious Lemon Bars

2 lemons
2 cups all-purpose flour
1 cup butter
½ cup powdered sugar
¼ teaspoon salt
1 cup granulated sugar
3 large eggs
⅓ cup fresh lemon juice
    Additional powdered sugar

1. Finely grate colored portion of lemon peel using bell grater or hand-held grater. Measure 4 teaspoons; set aside.

2. Preheat oven to 350°F. Grease 13×9-inch baking pan; set aside. Place 1 teaspoon lemon peel, flour, butter, ½ cup powdered sugar and salt in food processor. Process until mixture forms coarse crumbs.

3. Press mixture evenly in prepared pan. Bake 18 to 20 minutes or until golden brown.

4. Beat remaining 3 teaspoons lemon peel, granulated sugar, eggs and lemon juice in medium bowl with electric mixer at medium speed until well blended.

5. Pour mixture evenly over warm crust. Return to oven; bake 18 to 20 minutes longer or until center is set and edges are golden brown. Remove pan to wire rack; cool completely.

6. Dust with additional sifted powdered sugar; cut into 2×1½-inch bars.

7. Store tightly covered at room temperature. Do not freeze. *Makes 3 dozen bars*

Step 1. Grating lemon peel.

Step 3. Pressing crust mixture in 13×9-inch baking pan.

Step 5. Pouring lemon mixture over warm crust.

Harvest Pumpkin Cookies

2 cups all-purpose flour
1 teaspoon baking powder
1 teaspoon ground cinnamon
½ teaspoon baking soda
½ teaspoon salt
½ teaspoon ground allspice
1 cup butter, softened
1 cup sugar
1 cup canned pumpkin
1 large egg
1 teaspoon vanilla
1 cup chopped pecans
1 cup dried cranberries (optional)
  Pecan halves (about 36)

1. Preheat oven to 375°F.

2. Place flour, baking powder, cinnamon, baking soda, salt and allspice in medium bowl; stir to combine.

3. Beat butter and sugar in large bowl with electric mixer at medium speed until light and fluffy, scraping down side of bowl once. Beat in pumpkin, egg and vanilla. Gradually add flour mixture. Beat at low speed until well blended, scraping down side of bowl once. Stir in chopped pecans and cranberries with spoon.

4. Drop heaping tablespoonfuls of dough 2 inches apart onto *ungreased* cookie sheets. Flatten mounds slightly with back of spoon.

5. Press one pecan half into center of each mound. Bake 10 to 12 minutes or until golden brown.

6. Let cookies stand on cookie sheets 1 minute. Remove cookies with spatula to wire racks; cool completely.

7. Store tightly covered at room temperature or freeze up to 3 months.

Makes about 3 dozen cookies

Step 3. Stirring nuts and cranberries into dough.

Step 4. Dropping heaping tablespoonfuls of dough onto cookie sheet.

Step 5. Pressing pecan half into center of dough mound.

Gingerbread People

2¼ cups all-purpose flour
  2 teaspoons ground cinnamon
  2 teaspoons ground ginger
  1 teaspoon baking powder
  ½ teaspoon salt
  ¼ teaspoon ground cloves
  ¼ teaspoon ground nutmeg
  ¾ cup butter, softened
  ½ cup firmly packed light brown
    sugar
  ½ cup dark molasses
  1 large egg
    Red hot cinnamon candies
      (optional)
    Icing (page 84)
    Assorted food coloring
      (optional)
    Assorted candies and decors
      for decorating

1. Place flour, cinnamon, ginger, baking powder, salt, cloves and nutmeg in large bowl; stir to combine.

2. Beat butter and brown sugar in large bowl with electric mixer at medium speed until light and fluffy, scraping down side of bowl once. Beat in molasses and egg. Gradually add flour mixture. Beat at low speed until well blended, scraping down side of bowl once.

3. Form dough into 3 discs; wrap in plastic wrap and refrigerate 1 hour or until firm.

4. Preheat oven to 350°F. Working with 1 disc at a time, unwrap dough and place on lightly floured surface. Roll out dough with lightly floured rolling pin to ³/₁₆-inch thickness.

5. Cut out gingerbread people with floured 5-inch cookie cutters.

6. Place cutouts on *ungreased* cookie sheets. Press red hot cinnamon candies into dough for eyes or coat buttons.

7. Gently press dough trimmings together; reroll and cut out more cookies. (Rerolled dough will produce slightly tougher cookies than first rolling.)

continued on page 84

Step 4. Rolling out dough to ³/₁₆-inch thickness.

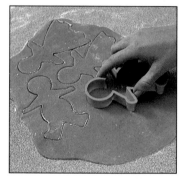

Step 5. Cutting dough with floured cookie cutters.

Step 7. Pressing dough trimmings together.

Gingerbread People, continued

8. Bake about 12 minutes or until edges are golden brown. Let cookies stand on cookie sheets 1 minute. Remove cookies with spatula to wire racks; cool completely.

9. Prepare Icing. Icing may be divided into small bowls and tinted with food coloring to use for decorative piping.

10. Place each colored Icing in small resealable plastic freezer bag. Cut off tiny corner of bag.

11. Pipe Icing decoratively onto cooled cookies; press candies in Icing. Let stand at room temperature 20 minutes or until set.

12. Store tightly covered at room temperature or freeze up to 3 months.

Makes about 16 large cookies

Icing*

1½ cups sifted powdered sugar
  2 tablespoons milk plus additional
      if needed
½ teaspoon vanilla

*Prepared creamy or gel-type frostings in tubes may be substituted for Icing, if desired.

Place all ingredients in medium bowl; stir with spoon until thick, but spreadable. (If Icing is too thick, stir in 1 teaspoon additional milk.)

Step 10. Cutting off tiny corner of bag.

Step 11. Piping Icing onto cooled cookies.

Icing: Checking consistency of Icing.

Gingerbread House

5¼ cups all-purpose flour
1 tablespoon ground ginger
2 teaspoons baking soda
1½ teaspoons ground allspice
1 teaspoon salt
2 cups firmly packed dark brown
    sugar
1 cup plus 2 tablespoons butter or
    margarine, softened
¾ cup dark corn syrup
2 large eggs
    Royal Icing (page 86)
    Assorted gum drops, hard
      candies and decors for
      decorating
    Powdered sugar (optional)

1. Draw patterns for house on cardboard, using diagrams on page 86 as guides; cut out patterns.

2. Preheat oven to 375°F. Grease large cookie sheet; set aside.

3. Place flour, ginger, baking soda, allspice and salt in medium bowl; stir to combine.

4. Beat brown sugar and butter in large bowl with electric mixer at medium speed until light and fluffy, scraping down side of bowl once. Beat in corn syrup and eggs. Gradually add flour mixture. Beat at low speed until well blended, scraping down side of bowl once.

5. Roll about ¼ of dough directly onto prepared cookie sheet to ¼-inch thickness. Lay sheet of waxed paper over dough. Place patterns over waxed paper 2 inches apart. Cut dough around patterns with sharp knife; remove waxed paper. Reserve scraps to reroll with next batch of dough.

6. Bake 15 minutes or until no indentation remains when cookie is lightly touched in center. While cookies are still hot, place cardboard pattern lightly over cookie; trim edges with sharp knife to straighten. Let stand on cookie sheet 5 minutes. Remove cookies with spatula to wire racks; cool completely. Repeat with remaining pattern pieces.

continued on page 86

Step 1. Drawing patterns for house.

Step 5. Placing patterns over waxed paper on dough.

Step 6. Trimming edges of cookies to straighten.

Gingerbread House, continued

7. Prepare Royal Icing. Some Icing may be divided into small bowls and tinted with food coloring to use for decorative piping.

8. Cover 12-inch square piece of heavy cardboard with aluminum foil to use as base for house.

9. Place Icing in small resealable plastic freezer bag. Cut off tiny corner of bag. Pipe Icing on edges of all pieces including bottom; "glue" house together at seams and onto base.

10. Pipe door, shutters, etc. onto front of house. Decorate as desired with Icing and candies. Dust house with sifted powdered sugar to resemble snow. *Makes 1 gingerbread house*

Royal Icing

1 egg white,* at room temperature
2 cups sifted powdered sugar
½ teaspoon almond extract

*To separate egg, see step 3 on page 46. Use only grade A clean, uncracked egg.

Beat egg white in small bowl with electric mixer at high speed until foamy. Gradually add 2 cups powdered sugar and almond extract. Beat at low speed until moistened. Increase mixer speed to high and beat until Icing is stiff.

Step 9. "Gluing" pieces of house together.

Step 10. Piping shutters onto house.

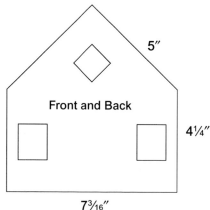

5″

Front and Back

4¼″

7³⁄₁₆″

Front: Cut 1 pattern for front of house. Cut 2 windows.

Back: Cut 1 pattern for back of house. Cut 2 windows. Cut 1 diamond.

6³⁄₁₆″

Sides: Cut 2 patterns.

4⁵⁄₁₆″

7¾″

Roof: Cut 2 patterns.

6¹⁄₁₆″

Christmas Ornament Cookies

Cookies
2¼ cups all-purpose flour
 ¼ teaspoon salt
 1 cup granulated sugar
 **¾ cup butter or margarine,
   softened**
 1 large egg
 1 teaspoon vanilla
 1 teaspoon almond extract
   Assorted candies or decors

Icing
 2 cups sifted powdered sugar
 2 tablespoons milk or lemon juice
   Assorted food coloring

1. For Cookies, place flour and salt in medium bowl; stir to combine.

2. Beat granulated sugar and butter in large bowl with mixer at medium speed until fluffy; scrape bowl once. Beat in egg, vanilla and almond extract. Gradually add flour mixture. Beat at low speed until well blended; scrape bowl once. Form dough into 2 discs; wrap in plastic wrap and refrigerate 30 minutes or until firm.

3. Preheat oven to 350°F. Place 1 disc on lightly floured surface. Roll out dough with lightly floured rolling pin to ¼-inch thickness. Cut dough into desired shapes with floured cookie cutters. Place cutouts on *ungreased* cookie sheets. Using drinking straw or tip of sharp knife, cut a hole near top of each cookie. Gently press dough trimmings together; reroll and cut out more cookies.

4. Bake 10 to 12 minutes or until edges are golden brown. Let cookies stand on cookie sheets 1 minute. Remove cookies with spatula to wire racks; cool completely.

5. For Icing, place powdered sugar and milk in small bowl; stir with spoon until smooth. If desired, Icing may be divided into small bowls and tinted with food coloring.

6. Place each colored Icing in small resealable plastic freezer bag. Cut off tiny corner of each bag. Pipe Icing decoratively onto cookies. Decorate with candies as desired. Let stand until set. Thread ribbon through cookie hole to hang as Christmas tree ornament.

Makes about 2 dozen cookies

Step 3. Cutting hole near top of cookie.

Step 6. Decorating cookies with candies.

Ukrainian Rolled Cookies (Siaroppskuake)

1 cup firmly packed light brown sugar
¾ cup shortening or margarine
⅓ cup dark molasses
2 large eggs
2 tablespoons finely grated lemon peel*
3 to 3½ cups all-purpose flour
1 teaspoon baking powder
1 teaspoon baking soda

*To grate lemon peel, see step 1 on page 78.

1. Beat brown sugar and shortening in large bowl with electric mixer at medium speed until light and fluffy, scraping down side of bowl once. Beat in molasses, eggs and lemon peel until well blended, scraping down side of bowl once.

2. Gradually add 3 cups flour, baking powder and baking soda. Beat at low speed until well blended, scraping down side of bowl once. Stir in additional flour with spoon until stiff dough forms. Form dough into 2 discs; wrap in plastic wrap and refrigerate until firm, 1 hour or overnight.

3. Preheat oven to 375°F. Grease 3 cookie sheets; set aside.

4. Working with 1 disc at a time, unwrap dough and place on lightly floured surface. Roll out dough with lightly floured rolling pin to ⅛-inch-thick rectangle. Cut dough with floured 2¾-inch star or scalloped cookie cutter. Place cutouts ½ inch apart on prepared cookie sheets.

5. Gently press dough trimmings together; reroll and cut out more cookies. (Rerolled dough will produce slightly tougher cookies than first rolling.)

6. Bake 7 to 8 minutes or until lightly browned around edges. Remove cookies with spatula to wire racks; cool completely.

7. Store tightly covered at room temperature or freeze up to 3 months.

Makes about 8 dozen cookies

Step 2. Stirring in additional flour.

Step 4. Cutting dough with floured cookie cutter.

Step 5. Pressing dough trimmings together.

Welsh Tea Cakes

¾ cup chopped dried mixed fruit,
   chopped dried mixed fruit
   bits or golden raisins
2 tablespoons brandy or cognac
2¼ cups all-purpose flour
2½ teaspoons ground cinnamon,
   divided
1 teaspoon baking powder
½ teaspoon baking soda
¼ teaspoon salt
¼ teaspoon ground cloves
1 cup butter, softened
1¼ cups sugar, divided
1 large egg
⅓ cup sliced almonds (optional)

1. Preheat oven to 375°F.

2. Combine dried fruit and brandy in medium bowl; let sit at least 10 minutes to plump fruit.

3. Place flour, 1½ teaspoons cinnamon, baking powder, baking soda, salt and cloves in medium bowl; stir to combine.

4. Beat butter and 1 cup sugar in large bowl with electric mixer at medium speed until light and fluffy, scraping down side of bowl once. Beat in egg. Gradually add flour mixture. Beat at low speed until well blended, scraping down side of bowl once. Stir in fruit and brandy with spoon.

5. Combine remaining ¼ cup sugar and 1 teaspoon cinnamon in small bowl. Roll heaping teaspoonfuls of dough into 1-inch balls; roll in cinnamon sugar to coat. Place balls 2 inches apart on *ungreased* cookie sheets.

6. Flatten each ball to ¼-inch thickness with bottom of glass dipped in sugar. Press 3 almond slices horizontally in center of each cookie. (Almonds will spread evenly and flatten upon baking.)

7. Bake 10 to 12 minutes or until lightly browned. Remove tea cakes with spatula to wire racks; cool completely.

8. Store tightly covered at room temperature or freeze up to 3 months.

Makes about 3½ dozen tea cakes

Step 2. Pouring brandy over dried fruit.

Step 5. Rolling dough balls in cinnamon sugar.

Step 6. Pressing almond slices in center of cookie.

INDEX